The Role of the Moon

poems

D.S. Martin

"... digest, / My soul, this wholesome meditation ..."
—John Donne

IRON PEN

PARACLETE PRESS
BREWSTER, MASSACHUSETTS

2025 First Printing

The Role of the Moon: Poems

ISBN 979-8-89348-017-7

Library of Congress Cataloging-in-Publication Data
Names: Martin, D. S. (Don) author
Title: The role of the moon : poems / D.S. Martin.
Description: Brewster, Massachusetts : Iron Pen, Paraclete Press, [2025] |
Summary: "These poems engage in a lyrical dialogue with the metaphysical poets. Themes of redemption, loss, renewal, and wonder permeate these verses, illuminating spiritual questions that have endured across ages"-- Provided by publisher.
Identifiers: LCCN 2025016884 (print) | LCCN 2025016885 (ebook) | ISBN 9798893480177 trade paperback | ISBN 9798893480184 epub
Subjects: LCSH: Metaphysics--Poetry | BISAC: POETRY / Subjects & Themes / Inspirational & Religious | RELIGION / Christianity / Literature & the Arts | LCGFT: Philosophical poetry
Classification: LCC PR9199.3.M3857 R65 2025 (print) | LCC PR9199.3.M3857 (ebook) | DDC 811/.54--dc23/eng/20250521
LC record available at https://lccn.loc.gov/2025016884
LC ebook record available at https://lccn.loc.gov/2025016885

10 9 8 7 6 5 4 3 2 1

Published by Paraclete Press

Brewster, Massachusetts

www.paracletepress.com

Printed in the United States of America

contents

–three–

–four–

–five–

– six –

– seven –

—appendix—

—acknowledgements—

a note concerning metaphysical poetry

The poems in this collection arose from meditations on the poetry of George Herbert and John Donne—and then from other seventeenth-century Metaphysical Poets (such as Henry Vaughan, Andrew Marvell, Thomas Traherne, Richard Crashaw, and Joseph Beaumont). It is hardly a clear category, but Metaphysical Poets to me simply mean those who use metaphors—sometimes elaborate, extensive metaphors known as conceits—to talk about ideas outside of human sense perception. Because these poets were deeply dedicated to their Christian faith—Herbert, Donne, and Traherne being Anglican priests—much of their poetry expresses their wrestlings with God, and with their own weaknesses.

John Donne's Holy Sonnets have long been of deep significance to me. The nineteen poems identified as Metaphysicals in this collection are my interactions with Donne's nineteen Holy Sonnets—where I, in turn, wrestle with the transcendental.

Other seventeenth-century poets I have interacted with here include Ben Jonson, John Milton, and William Shakespeare—even though they are not considered Metaphysical poets. The impulse to reflect on intangibles through the use of metaphors is hardly restricted to the seventeenth century, and so I also found myself responding to the work of such giants as Gerard Manley Hopkins, Elizabeth Barrett Browning, and Emily Dickinson.

Would it be a stretch to describe my new poems, and those of poets like me, as being New Metaphysicals? I would be honoured if you found this suggestion fitting.

Soli Deo Gloria,

DSM

ANOTHER AMPERSAND (+&)

What I further love about the humble ampersand
that former   twenty seventh letter of the alphabet
is its grace   & how   despite
its relative anonymity   it communicates
not needing its name spoken   per se   or even known
like the Corinthian vase painter
identified only by the ampersand tail-flourish of his sphinx
& like the unnamed angel   directing Philip
down the road to Gaza   & Philip   himself
an obscure clay vase   brimming with good news
& even the receptive Ethiopian   whatever his name was
& how the ampersand directs our attention
elsewhere   but unlike the snowplow driver
whose hidden impulse to leave his mark
bent a shopping cart   into a pretzelesque signature
stuck in the snow
for the ampersand is content
to connect all that's gone before   with what is yet to come
perhaps suggesting
that although we're also bent   & all so twisted
& stuck in the now   that that need not be
the final word

—one—

"With a mercy that outrides
The all of water, an ark
For the listener; for the lingerer with a love glides
Lower than death and the dark . . ."
—Gerard Manley Hopkins

GARDEN (Metaphysicals I)

This world is a garden   fearfully made
an unruly orchard   once well formed
though now decayed   I am a gardener
who mourns   well-meaning   overwhelmed

misguided   having let children run amuck
through border beds   They've torn
iris leaves for wispy swords   trampled stems
& muddied blooms beneath their rubber soles

I dare not look to left or right   Rodent holes
appear under fences   Wild winds have broken
branches   It's more than we can handle on our own
I despair of loss   It's all needing repair

You've made me   & this garden   & will your work
decay?   I'm a dried-out vegetable patch overrun
with weeds   an olive orchard filled with tears
I look to you   to conquer all my fears

RADIANT (Metaphysicals II)

Those who look to you are radiant

Sometimes I make the mistake   of being
too corporeal-minded   forgetting

we're predominantly made of light
missing how   like the moon's reflection in a pool

we've been made with you to shine
Even in the womb   we are luminously woven

& strands of what seem like moonbeams   twine
& retwine   within lambent bodies   all our lives

absorbed like bread & wine   into the bloodstream
Do I really know   how we taint the light we're given

& the darkling I'm capable of?   I fight
for every touch of your absent hand to be mine

Every drop of your presence   draws my thirst
to be built into a temple of light

WATER TOWER (Metaphysicals III)

In the heat of summer   as afternoon
wears on   as octogenarians care for
their flower gardens   & sprinklers jet

across expanses of lawn   the water
level   in the water tower   of each
little town   slowly goes down

So much of what I've been given
slips through my fingers   evaporates
into open air   goes down the drain

So much sweat   so many tears
over lesser desires I've aspired to
have weighted my prayers for years

with disgruntled   self-tickling sighs
over what has come to nothing
Yahweh   I pray now for rain

CARWASH (Metaphysicals IV)

Have you ever desired
a carwash for the soul   rushed
right up to those
retractable doors   to drive
right in   let the gush & spray
wash away   mud-splatters
& grease?   You knew   didn't you?
you'd still have to face   that bang
clang   under your hood

Have you ever desired
a soul mechanic?   You knew   didn't you?
you'd bristle at repair suggestions
implying your ride's no good

Imagine   if you can   a wrecking
yard   a refiner's fire   & a high-end
custom shop   all-in-one
where everything we are   & everything
we do   is made new   where the pitch-perfect roar
from your ignition   rings in
a cloudless spring evening   so cleanly

that freshly paved highways   spread to the horizon
& far beyond   for the likes of us
to glisten   among the stars

POEM FOR A TIME OF CRISIS

What is that small feathered thing
meek & knowing   that survived
in cramped quarters   with all that would
soon be released upon us?

Without fear   she lets me reach
deep into her now-lidless box
lift her in my hand   & feel
her gentle heart thrumming

Is she kin to the dove   Noah released from
his window   or the first robin of spring?
Those who have come through storms
will recognize her plumage

Like to the lark at break of day   she'll sing
We have not been left alone   Her belief
merges with mine   as I fling
her skyward   & watch her take wing

knowing she'll return with an olive leaf

CURVED BEAUTY

The seeds of geometry   as seen through flowers
& hives   through webs & shells   suggest
possibilities   beyond themselves almost made manifest
for the perfectly straight   infinite line   described by Mister Singh
in Math class

doesn't exist   Even a sunbeam starts with the sun
& either fades   or is broken   & what seems straight
admits variance   the horizon line   the shaft of a feather
the bowing branch   the bending river   none of which
goes on forever

Glory be to God   for the dance of willows in the wind
the swerve & swoop of swallows in flight   the arc
of a crescent moon   the curve of a tusk   the crook in a brook
the undulations in sand dunes   the refractions
& reflections of light

RIFF ON TRAHERNE

Without want   there could be no enjoyment
The grey man tramps winter roads
finds the seat by the hearth   the fresh
fragrance of steaming bread
from the farmhouse kitchen

There could be   no enjoyment without want
Rembrandt's light receives all the praise
but what of his shadows?
What could be drawn from his infants' deaths
from Saskia on her sickbed?

No enjoyment could there be   without want
What joy   in hearing Billie Holiday sing
without her sorrow?
Stirring   our every loss   since the womb
we borrow from her soaring

Could there be enjoyment without want?   No
distance to drive   means no arrival
We only see stars after dark
& eyes must acclimatize   when we walk
in from the daylight

Without want   no enjoyment   could be there
  beneath the spreading maple
    no pleasure in cool   without heat
  & for heaven to be heaven   our griefs
    must have risen   & suffered defeat

AS SHE FLEW PAST

As though in their own living room
the young couple conferred
& I tried to let their anonymity
& the fantasy of their privacy
last   having other things to do
in the labyrinth of this IKEA showroom
I did not hear a single word
until his rough voice drew
my ear   *At least I know enough*
not to marry you   My razored heart
felt like an empty sack   as she flew past
not looking back   & it felt even hollower
when no one tried to follow her

KITTY STOBLING DANCES ON

Who can discern what makes her take the chance
stilt-walking   precariously on a downtown street
a dance   to catch the eye of passersby
each upturned face   gawking questioningly?

They stop mid-step   surprised by her performance
a wonder   a conundrum   a curiosity
Is her love of unexpected grace   & the theatrical
what leaves her   risking absurdity?

Of these flat-footed rationalists   not one believes her
Come dance with Kitty Stobling   & dance with me
on mile-high stilts   half hidden by clouds
a high-flying myth   to help us all see

The rogues of the world   mock all that's beyond them
I'm mainly an observer   not smooth on my feet
but I dance in midair   where beauty walks   waiting
& the love of God stirs like wind in the wheat

Whirling & swirling   behind storm-formed clouds
graceful troops dance with Kitty   & all the tall trees
high above the timorous faces of the crowd
who never bother   with our identities

—two—

"Choose love not in the shallows but in the deep."

—Christina Rossetti

SIDEWALK CRACKS (Metaphysicals V)

I am a little world   made cunningly
whose every element   spirals
down   mirroring the world
outside   where glistening

surfaces fade   like a tarnished
crown   The planet prophesied
when I wasn't listening   through
sidewalk cracks   through

the scuffs   which mock my new
shoes   & through hatchet blades
grown dull   so I never heard
what was awaiting   my eye & ear

Though now I feel   the zeal in my
soul   like a late-night campfire
will fully burn out   unless
wilfully stoked & stirred

CLIMATOLOGY WITH AUGUSTINE

In rain shadow   where dry winds
bring no moisture   deserts form
When grains grow stinted   when cows
grow thin   when bins grow empty   famine begins
Just like bare metal   starting to rust
illness thrives in undernourished   anxious hearts
anxiety in insecure days   & insecurity
in the absence of trust

What kind of house
has rotting window frames
a crumbling wall?
What kind of home
fills its empty spaces
with sorrow?
A solitary voice
echoes down the hall

Ice forms on the shallow pond   as the day's
warmth   escapes into a cloudless sky
Where good is missing   its opposite will rise
as predictable   as prevailing winds from the west
Woe to the weak   & oppressed   who've no one
to lift their burden   & give them rest

INFERNO

Blessed is the fragile fortress of the forest floor
where the flare of fox fur   is enough to suggest

conflagration   where auburn needles fall
from a dry fir like flakes of snow   Dead branches break

in a high wind   & brittle sticks await
the careless flick from a cigarette   The flame

first birthed in a match   awakens with heat
where kindling's stored   takes fleet leaps

from birch to birch   where each leaf crumples
if scorched   yet will still fall if left to pay

the yellow cost of October's slow burn
as cool first creates loss   & cold soon fosters frost

MILES TO GO

On a snowy evening   returning
through the cold from town
with nothing sold   & nothing bought
the cart creaking its *I told you so*
along the ice-packed road   as flakes flitter down
like leaves   to hold the woods in snow
& weave their spell   his little horse stops
not because he's pulled her reins   but because
of nothing   his usual encouragement   absent
& she senses his need   to sweep
aside his grief   in the deep
calm of the roadside   He has no tranquility
despite what his poem later tells   for his return
is empty-handed   with Christmas near
& no ability to buy gifts for his wife   & their dear
children   with his life mirrored in the emptiness that dwells
in the dark woods   on this long long night of the solstice
where he uncontrollably weeps   over promises
he's unable to keep   & then Eunice   his mare
shakes her harness bells

NEW LIFE

It will flame out, like shining from shook foil . . .

—Gerard Manley Hopkins

Try your best to imagine the worst
a derelict   boarded-up   burned-out place
overtaken by weeds & waste   where crumbling concrete
& rusted junk rub desolation into whatever dreams first flowered
before despair toppled & devoured them

Or look across a scarred landscape
where wildfire   blackened & flattened forests
leaving a few charred sticks   where faint fence lines
& random bricks   declare what once flourished
in this boom & bust hinterland

Despite the damage we do   through malice
or neglect   the doom & dust passes   the fireweed
blueberries & grasses thrive   the hopeless vacuum fills
with new desire   & amid all that seems irredeemable
innocence comes alive

PALMLESS SUNDAY

for Henry Vaughan

Listen & hear
        the black basalt of Korazim
mourn   in deep resonant tones
what her citizens rejected
        The ecstatic white limestone
of Jerusalem   would also shout out
if the children's high cry
had been neglected

We'd then hear
        another *Hosanna*
provoked from a throatless throat
a joyous   mineral sound
rising from the ground
echoed in the distant sky
by gulls & seraphim
inviting hushed children to join in

RUINS REMIND US

What we do   rarely stays done
Not just laundry   & dishes
& the trimming of trees

Rembrandts require restoration
castle ramparts crumble   & scaffolds
arise   along cathedral walls

Remnants of Lamanai   & Tintern Abbey's
ruins   remind us   nothing remains
forever

Even the sharp edges of Donne's poems
are weathered by years of linguistic shift
in how our ears receive them

Along the Grand Canal they hide
the repairs in progress   behind clever
screens   What we do   rarely stays done

Even our love   will need continual
renewal   to keep our precious ones warm
after we're gone

THE CHANGE

for Franco & Maria

Where the little trickle normally cut across the road   where it normally
made its little rut   & sparkled over the dusty stretch   disappearing
under the rusty corrugated fence   by Franco & Maria's place

the rushing rivulet grew   The rains came down   while hurricane winds
thrashed palm branches   & flattened plantain   & the gush dug
its way into the gravel track   churning dirt & debris

undercutting whatever concrete there was   & then crashed
full-strength against their house   break & enter   without invitation
a brown flood   filled with broken branches   with whatever chunks of wood

torn from roofs & walls   were caught in its path   streaming   at first
ankle deep across the floor   & then more & more   nowhere for it to go
but right through their door   water overflowing the chicken coop

till every hen must be drowned   carrying everything in its way
down & down   into the ravine below   dirt & dishes   plastic pails
& dead dogs   & then the collapse must have come

& then the non-buoying reprieve   as floodwaters slowed
after having washed the family's life away   & there's no point
digging anything out of the mud   That's how it must have been

based on the things I've seen   foundations crumbled into rivers
That   & all the broken pieces surrounding this building site
for I couldn't ask details   with walls of language between us

José Luis & his crew   having already cleared rubble aside already
having poured the concrete pad   Maria & her neighbours
sit across the street   watching her house go up

a few Canadians labouring for free under a Dominican foreman
But then   my wife's invitation to participate comes   A son home from work
grabs a hammer   as the women & children paint siding

My Gloria   hugs each one   & Maria joyfully points heavenward
Hay cambio   proclaiming the change   They laugh & sing
every kid vying for a turn with the roller   carrying boards

learning how to measure   & mark   & hammer nails home
& looking up to José Luis   balanced on high rafters
& picturing a future   when some day   they might be like him

MY FINAL CREDITS (Metaphysicals VI)

I doubt my final credits
are quite ready to roll
though   so far

I've outlived John Donne's span
& that of so many of the poets
I admire   I can't refute

that   far too soon   mid-
sentence   I will expire
Gluttonous death

will make a meal of me
& divide body   from soul
make   perhaps   this very one

my last breath   last scene
last poem   which I hope
will be constructed well

Far more of my life's
in the take-up reel
than in what's to come

which is no cause for despair
as in anticipation   I prepare
for the sequel

—three—

"The cross of Christ . . . is a Tree set on fire with invisible flame that illuminateth all the World."

—Thomas Traherne

LINE & COLOUR

The first map you saw   was
mere line & colour   before
you knew to multiply it out into a world
before a blue curl   could be a river
& a straight thread   your street

You gradually heard three little squares
declare themselves houses   & three little trees
go further   & suggest a whole forest
& the forest   to suggest the wild   where lines
lost & overgrown   no longer meet

where things you cannot own
never lie down   confined to a legend
& the mysteries of darkness
& light   remain unknown
where those trees   those same little trees

rise high above two-dimensional paper
to be blown   in the uncharted wind
just as we   will be shown
how the landscape   too   in all its line & colour
reveals far more than itself

YOU COULD HAVE MADE (Sonnet 4)

You could have made the worlds grey & lopsided
a monochrome for flora   sky & sea
but your precision made sure none collided
you framed the tiger's fearful symmetry
I learn about you from the things you've made
although my thoughts are tentative at best
the peace   the turbulence   both sun & shade
& lean upon your book to learn the rest
But even in your word you speak unclearly
conundrums of both holy wars & grace
I try to make the ways of God to merely
make sense   so I won't fall flat on my face
It seems you'd rather prove my proofs untrue
so I will turn from certainties to you

I DRAW IN DUST A CIRCLE WITH MY FOOT

George Herbert's "Perirrhanterium" 44 & 56

I draw in dust a circle with my foot
Instead of counting what's
inside I'm stuck on what is not

Why feel struck down a worm
made worse by praise for lesser work?
My heart & head project

my projects high but won't equate
my worth with what I've done or strive
with those I cannot hope to emulate

Spurred on in each attempt to start afresh
I draw in dust a circle with my foot
a contemplation on eternity

which mocks the scribblings I make on this page
I ache with joy in all I try to grasp
then will accept *the gifts reserved for age*

MERCIES

after Donne's "Occasional Mercies"

How curious it is
wrapped in rags of time
for a child   in the depth of night
to text her sorrows
to a school friend
on the planet's sunlit side
& receive an instant reply

How long her legs become
on the sky bridge   striding
from winter   into the summer
of Caribbean sunlight   where
fruit is ripe in season

Her plane might pass over
both desert & ocean   before
touching down   She oversteps
spring   then oversteps autumn
on the return flight
back & forth   from south to north
for the heat coexists with cold
as day with night

When she's benighted   wintered
frozen   clouded   & eclipsed
forgetful of eternal noon
what seems as bright as the moon?
But Love's legs are stronger
& so much longer   simultaneously
bringing justice & mercy
with no sign   of spring or fall
gradual dusk   or gradual dawn

IMAGINED CORNERS (Metaphysicals VII)

Take the globe by her imagined
corners   & stretch her flat
like evening   against the sky
Blow your trumpets   angels
to stir   our souls
& stir bodies that have died

Call Bethlehem's innocents   & those
drowned in seas   those
ploughed under in battle
by a drum beat   those
trapped in the tower   those
first responders   those shaken
by marauders   those taken
by disease   those burned
at the stake   those spectacle
watchers   who lasted little
longer   & every girl
time turned   from a fragrant
flower into one   whose bent brittle
stem   bowed her   to the grave

Gather each decomposed husk   for
no matter how scattered   each must
recompose   as our souls must
respond   to all we're given
& grip   beyond our grasp
this new call to worship

SHEPHERD (Sonnet 5)

On clear cold nights when far stars speckle skies
& wood smoke goes straight up & disappears
a dozen constellations   to my eyes
are dull blurs   when I think back through the years
to when the angel spoke to us that night
joined by the brilliant vast angelic choir
which overcame our senses with such light
& planted in each man the same desire
that prodded us till we reached Bethlehem
& led us to an unmarked cattle shed
We stumbled in and startled both of them
those parents   by the baby's manger bed
The townsfolk were astounded by our story
of uncouth shepherds blessed to see God's glory

SIMEON (Sonnet 6)

Rough men   though at their work   were first to hear it
They were not looking   but were first to see
Although I'm old & close to death   the Spirit
revealed that God would show the child to me
I waited till the Spirit whispered when
then to the temple with no hesitation
I went   & watched as parents carried in
their newborn sons for sacred dedication
I sensed before too long   some would be dead
when Bethlehem is ravaged by the sword
but then I saw him   & I bowed my head
& in my hands I held our tiny Lord
Now I depart in peace   desire of nations
my wondering eyes have now seen God's salvation

STARGAZER (Sonnet 7)

From my high tower   first I saw it rise
the harbinger   portending divine birth
a bright horizon star in the night skies
announcing heaven coming down to earth
Our caravan   soon followed trade routes west
in search of a grand palace for this king
but over a poor town it came to rest
& local prophecies said the same thing
Would it be safe for us to see his face
or would such glory strike us to our death?
We each brought gifts with us   in a jewelled case
& knelt before the door   & held our breath
His mother laughed with joy when we inquired
To worship the God-child   all we desired

A POET AVAILABLE FOR GOD'S SERVICE

El Cibao, Dominican Republic

Empty-handed except for the hands
themselves   & the narrow skill
that trickles through them   like rain
splishing through a sandy gutter
just as I am   I come

I come   observing a rivulet's course
across pebbles   & the ravine below
for the swimming of sons & daughters
which is both   where
each home's waste drains   & their source
of drinking water

In crafting words I have some strength   but
only pull out a pencil to mark the length
where each board is to be cut
as we rebuild this family's home   I come
unburdened by opinions of how to complete the task
just doing what I'm asked   until it's done

Even eight months later   the poem I return with
is useless to share with those whose English is so thin
Empty-handed again   I come
Without reputation   paper or pen
I grab a hungry shovel   & rhythmically apply its bite
to moving one more pile of gravel

—four—

"Bring us, O Lord God, at our last awakening
into the house and gate of heaven. . . ."
—John Donne

PRAYER

-I-

Paraclete   I have no resources
for picturing
            your purposeful presence on the face
of the deep   before the formless world
took shape   Still   I embrace

the mystery   turbulence stirring dark waters
where no sunlight/moonlight/starlight had ever shone
& where the roving
of a human eye   requiring light   had never gone

-II-

The three-way conversation   permitting
what had already found existence in your thoughts   began
so that what appeared   seems not so much like some new jazz riff
pouring forth   or unplanned colours & shapes gradually growing
on some vast canvas
               but the manifestation of the inevitable
as you had scooped it from limitless chaos

in the windless whirling of eternity past

& had already pronounced it *good*

-III-

My anthropomorphizing imagination   transposes such joyful grandeur

into comic-book pretentiousness   thundering voices solemnly

commanding the already-eager elements   to be

But with no human ear to hear   the Word need not

have made a sound   The Word

who was with God   who was God   & is God

& evermore shall be the one & only god   may have spoken

silently   before there was anything to vibrate

or for it to vibrate upon

-IV-

I think of the image

                    you made us in

hand-molded   smooth-polished

                    her & him

beyond bodily appearance
                    our position

now cracks & crumbles
                    & grows dim

-V-

In the cool of the evening you walked   Yahweh
with the naked gardener   when your shade
made the blaze of the perfectly placed sun less intense
& you smiled at how he chose to prefer one good
above another
            although you knew   didn't you
after a while   he would choose to turn away?

In the cool of the morning   Yahweh   you smile
at my attempts at understanding   & these little
turns of phrase I offer up
in the garden patch I try to tend

-VI-

You are the ever-alert god   El Roi

beneath desert skies   you hear my cries
where your people   have driven   & driven me out
as though I were a scraggly goat
not one with a clank-bell   to be retrieved
nor the flawless one   that escaped
to the wild   but the scrawny   thorn-scraped
rejected one   struggling into pitiful bush-shade

-VII-

You are the all-sufficient one   El Shaddai
I walk before you   along no distinguishable path
straining ears for your whispered voice   *Did your staff*
just tap my shoulder? You don't reply
You're like a father   toying with his infant son
I wheel about   & recognize your laugh
in the predictable way you unpredictably provide
as   exactly-what-I-want   almost comes

-VIII-

Sometimes I hear you in the back garden   or in
the long-shadowed morning
                    when the house is still
when my day's walk has not yet collided with your will

& I almost see the blooming Rose of Sharon
                    as a sign
I'm the one to start
                    our one-sided talks
I'm the one to say *Amen*   It's hard to not want to shoehorn
your spirit into some box of my own design
when you make a temple of my God-battered heart
when you leave it to me to begin again

-IX-

You govern the galaxies   Adonai   so what claim have I
on your attention?   O mighty Elohim
why are you mindful of us at all?   Taking one step down
from the angels   you honoured us   making
yourself in our smudged image   reaching
down   to play in our sandbox   leaving
the necessary work of praise   to rocks & trees
since we remain distracted
                    What in you
made making us   worthwhile?
You shepherd the shepherd   & wrestle the wrestler
You smile when I get anything right
even when I've questioned if you cared
                              Your caravan

of perfect love   reaches beyond
perfection   following your own stars
through the night   as though sailing a sea of sand
to pause   for a hastily prepared meal
by a Bedouin tent   where again you smile
as your bounty is shared

-X-

I will try to not pretend   Abba Father
          that having found favour
               in your sight   implies I'm getting it right
that you approve my quick answers
to slow questions
                    my bulldozing of the meek
                                   I cry to you
El Elyon with no resources
for holiness of my own
                         & understand
I have no way to remove the stains   as I wipe juice
from my chin   on the back of my hand

Lord   I pray
                              Love   love me do
since my wisest prayers   are those
you've already granted   & taught me to seek

GLORIFIED (Metaphysicals VIII)

No longer bent   like weighted
branches   or shrivelled   like apples
in the bottom of a bushel basket
No longer circling & recircling
in unsolvable mental labyrinths   my parents
have left all muddled perceptions behind
Now they shine   like towers   night-clad in spotlight
like stars visible in the morning sky   like uplifted crowns
flashing   reflections of the Father
& my grandparents   too   no longer locked
in history   have leapt beyond
the limits of every age
Who sees me stumbling heavenward
laughs   gasps at my time-bound ways?
Might faithful souls   now glorified
bother more than a glimpse?
Or are they fixed on the source of all that light?

IMPLEMENT

after Emily Dickinson

Imagine an implement that permits
you to reach   further than you
otherwise could   flinging your

speech   further than megaphone
telephone   or internet ever would
to breach the high atmosphere

to where there's no gravity or air
so your words are heard even in God's ear
through the apparatus   of prayer

THE ROLE OF THE MOON (Metaphysicals IX)

I play the part of an earthbound
stone   you   the role of the moon
in this silent   ceaseless   standoff
As a rock   an oversized pebble
I'm kicked along some city sidewalk
rolling into a ditch   from which
I see the curve of your shoulder
turned away   high   beyond wispy clouds
If I could be a monument
or stone floor   where bent knees bleed
might I gain your notice?
If I were bolder   I'd cry out
complain of your inattention
yet who am I to dispute?   You know
me   as well as you knew the hand
reaching for the fruit
If I were a mountain   or craggy
coast   would you command me
to fall into the sea?   Could I dare pray
with your face full on me?
Your distance is just a pose   mine
a fallacy   I think it mercy
that you feign to turn away

PRIDE BE NOT DEATH (Metaphysicals X)

Pride   be not death   for as I've
stretched to reach out from these
brambles   to cut away the vines
about my ankles   to step out on this
promontory   you swell in me
like a boxer's battered nose

distorted & off-colour   You flutter
like a fledgling finch   demanding
the attention of its mother
You buff yourself to shine
like a showroom convertible   destined
for the wrecking yard   But still I grasp

for you   a rope to grab & release
hand over hand   a welcome provision
a helpful infatuation   a healthy garden
becoming greener   & fuller
& overgrown   entangling my feet
& pulling me down

SARGASSUM

after George Herbert's "Denial" (Punta Cana)

Your ears are not so filled
with crashing waves   or the merengue
the girl behind the beach-front bar
sings along to   in Spanish
as to not   hear my prayers

You're like the colourful fish
swimming teasingly
within arms' reach   as we snorkel
yet completely untouchable
You're like the trees
filled with cattle heron   just beyond
the resort's boundary fence

May the invisible wall   my devotion
faces   be like the immense
reddish-brown barrier of wave-tossed
sargassum   between beach & ocean
we easily step across

THIS CORONET (Sonnet 8)

after Andrew Marvell

Subjected to disgraces every day
from those like me who claim to follow him
my Saviour's head will still not turn away
from injuries inflicted by my sin
There is no garland to redress these wrongs
not even if I write a flawless sonnet
or play like Beiderbecke melodious songs
at Heaven's gate upon a golden cornet
For when an artist intricately weaves
a chaplet for the king from tender strands
she pictures her own head with laurel leaves
Our offerings are tainted by our hands
This coronet which I think now adorns
my Saviour's head keeps turning into thorns

WEIGHT (Metaphysicals XI)

    How can we stomp it out?
        all the rude   crude
smashed glass & heartache
        the grabbing   stabbing
fussing   & fuming
    Sledgehammers just break
fingers   Unset bones
won't heal straight   Is it worth
all it would take to mend?
    Those trapped   & unreleased
send acid into their bellies   spread
grief thinly into the world
    but my corrosion singes heaven
bends its floorboards
with the weight of all I ask
    The Infinite   is infinitely
up to the task

PRAYER WITHOUT ANSWER

There was the time   when far more than two
or three of us gathered   & though I'm sure
you were among us   you didn't let on

I was thinking   I needed my faith stirred
like the sugary concoction   bubbling
in the jam pot   swirling to the surface
with every twist of my wooden spoon
strawberry redolence   rising in the air
but nothing sweet came   & death
seemed undeterred

So   once again   you heard my prayer
against disease   against the odds
against one narrow doom

There was the time at the hospice   & the time
at the hospital   & time after time
in so many living rooms   when to say   *No Lord*
would have been to horribly presume
pulling Leviathan in with a fishhook
as my response   to unresponsive cancer

On our friends' back deck   as my heart
half-guilty-for-health   cries out
knowing   here & now
we have no answer   & that this
isn't the end
together   before you   we bow

—*five*—

“With thee / O let me rise / As larks, harmoniously, /
And sing this day thy victories: / Then shall the fall
further the flight in me.”

—George Herbert

BIRD-WATCHING WITH CONFUCIUS

The beginning of wisdom   Confucius said
is to call things by their proper name   & so
as I watch the feeder   I learn to discern
sparrows from finches   amid their flickering
& bickering   & scattering of seed
& by this   seek to sound wiser   if only to myself

But perhaps there's confusion
& he really meant   *the beginning*
of knowledge   for the plumage of words
overlaps & ruffles   with flap & vibrato

As I observe circling birds
            the black-capped chickadee
            & dark-eyed junco
whose need for feed   I've heard   is met by God
& kind retirees   I hope to find
the beginning of wisdom   through such things

A bird doesn't fear   her branch breaking
Confucius said   *because she trusts in her wings*

SPARROW (Metaphysicals XII)

Obscurely yet surely backyard birds
simple & further from corruption with
the wonder of wings call us to praise

A sparrow caught & fluttering in the
mechanism of the feeder's perch
gave a forlorn cry & lay still

resigned to futility Carefully I
reached a gloved hand to manoeuvre
her free concerned her injuries fatal

Wondernumb to their comings &
goings I was still struck as her
loosened body shockingly gone

to a distant tree needed no pause
for recovery doing then & always
as she is called to do

CARDINAL VIRTUES

So with these, since there are four,
we must look for them in the same way.
—Plato's *Republic*, Book IV

I am no ornithologist   or even a
temperate bird watcher   being so
quickly called away by the urgency of
interests
                    but I have noticed
when the cardinal makes a *prudent*
chit-chit   he   or even the elusive she
is checking out the feeder   & will soon
alight
              Later   from the secluded cedar
his song's more full-throated   & bright
despite the *fortitude* he needs   to
establish their territory   in these
adjoining yards
                              I googled it   He
sings divergent songs   to guard
the nest   announce arrival   to tell his
mate of food   or danger   or warn of
cardinal *justice* to any trespassing stranger

POEM ARISING FROM A LINE BY HERBERT (Sonnet 9)

I am in all a weak   disabled thing
a bird with broken wing   a stringless bow
for though   I strive to make much of my skill
your will seems to negate all that I do
Will you someday permit this bird to fly?
Lift to the sky an arrow from my hand?
Let what I've planned   bring honour to your name
so I won't blame myself   for wasting hours
All powers in me   originate in you
All that I do   is meant to bring you praise
My days I pour out   like a singing bird
whose song's unheard   despite how well it's sung
This work you have begun   bring to completion
then from my heart   I'll say   *Your will be done*

WATCHER OF THE FIELDS

There's one who watches the fields
& another who watches the watcher
of the fields
As we drive north or west
beyond the populated part of town
I suddenly see & point
but you've no chance to glance up
before the car roof blocks your view
Another time you're the one
pointing & I'm the one pointlessly
scanning the roadside for proof
of what's past
The watcher watching from the
highest vantage point a form of
greater proportion than so many
lesser things
Those scurriers & flutterers
oblivious much as we are to such
bright wings

PEREGRINE FALCON (Sonnet 10)

now thou but stoop'st to me

— Ben Jonson

The falcon like a teardrop heaven cries
from higher than the city's tallest tower
designed to fall precisely through clear skies
now hurtles at two hundred miles per hour
At such a speed what keeps her flashing eyes
from drying out her lungs from ripping open?
She's been made fast but pigeons were made wise
at least enough to dodge a diving falcon

But you O Lord are like a bird of prey
whose talons I would not try to resist
When caught I will not try to get away
when held by you I'll pray that you'll persist
O hold me Lord while I am here below
then lift me up for I'll be glad to go

OWL HEART

His heart is an owl   was once a-strum
with silent sovereignty   swinging low   coming forth
over shadowy vole-grass   mouse-grass
each blade a-trembling   like rodent ears   numb
with fear   that hear no sound   but sense a presence
like warm little nostrils lifted too late
snatched up & carried home to the nest   was once
familiar only with fulfilment   a concert of terror
thick neck   winged shoulders   ready talons
& with binocular sight   piercing the night
rendered the hidden exposed   was once
the ultimate predator   descending from the unknown
swallowing prey whole   absorbing flesh & blood
coughing up pellets of fur & bone
as insatiable as the grave

His heart is a Mountsberg owl   no longer free to roam
ever since a swoop to scoop   some morsel
from the roadway   he was caught in a glare
as bright as noonday   a blare to out-thunder thunder
& a rolling planet bearing down to drag him under
making one wing into a broken branch

limp with crackling brown leaves

leaving him a feathered spectre

with a diminished range   chain-link encaged

& exposed to the curious stare

of schoolgirls through the fence   where his only defence

is to drown them   in the still yellow pools

of his eyes

OSPREY

Like with the osprey   reflected
        in a misty lake
the elegant figure   passing
        first one window
        then another
        in an upstairs room
the elusive moon
        not fully showing her face
we often know more
        than we can prove

We watch her move
        moon   woman   bird
abide in the knowledge
        of the half   or almost seen
the whispers   we know
        we've never heard
the longing   for what yet
        has never been

A WINDOW

A window is not as open as it seems
keeping out cold
        the pine needles' freshness
        the cardinal's call

A starling dives straight for it
veering off
        last second
when its gold surface gleams

Not as open as it seems   like the job posting
soon filled by the boss's daughter
the chimney whose nest is only discovered
when smoke fills the room

A window is not as open as it seems
        & in the kitchen   steams
        when we're boiling water
becoming clouded

Not as open or   perhaps   as clear
somewhat like the accidental click of a door

behind you   a minnow trap with no way out
a blind eye   a deaf ear

You can see the traffic on the river's far shore
but the bridge is a long way down
The hungry turtle prods your finger
through aquarium glass

A window is not as open as it seems
as darkness advances   the outer world
is lost to its mirror   & we're strangely
on display to passersby

The old man listens to the pastor's words
He smiles & nods   smiles & nods

—six—

"God's gifts put man's best dreams to shame."

—Elizabeth Barrett Browning

CHORUS OF THE SPLENDID POISON FROG

Oophaga speciosa

With its saw-like rhythm   you once could hear our chorus
the chitter-chitter-chit   like a painted   grit-filled gourd
shaken by a child   the winding of a timeless clock   sifting
through the rainforest
                                        Like the last of last year's crop
of tiny tomatoes   long gone   from dried-out vines
we will not be found   Our astounding rich redness
always was a warning sign   protection from predators
who'd otherwise   open wide   so we'd really no reason to hide

Search the mountains of Panama   turn over every new leaf
every stone   on stony ground   Never again will our toes
splayed wide on each foot   secure our place
You're too late   we're extinct   kaput
                                                            Like wisdom   who cried
yet was disregarded for so long   our calls are no longer heard
we're gone   If you call   we will make no sound   until
perhaps   all things are made new   Like all creation   we wait

REFLECTION ON SHAKESPEARE'S SONNET 146

O   my poor soul
the eternal has never seemed in need
of time   & so   outward things steal
my inward eye
        making a name   for an image
an image for a name   a house to hold
what houses seem to claim

We were talking   about the space
between us all   & how extravagantly
I paint exterior walls   though I know
within   lies my soul's shortfall

O   my soul   I pour
my strengths   where they
will often spill   & spend
what I can little afford
on what comes to an end
Within be fed   without be rich no more

THE WORLD'S LAST NIGHT (Metaphysicals XIII)

If tonight were the world's last night
might I spend it striking the anvil
of rhetoric to prod wanderers to
become insiders?
Might I pester God to open his
doors slightly wider?
Might I quietly sip wine
with my sweet wife or keep
wrestling alone in what Yeats calls
my quarrel with myself?
As I cross the threshold
from one gift to another
leaving whirlwinds behind
will regret slip away as I find
my small faith is all I have
to lay before the throne?

THE WORLD'S SHARPNESS

arising from the 24th sonnet of Elizabeth Barrett Browning

Despite a handstitched receiving blanket
for your arrival soft dry & warm
& your mother's strong arms
despite the appearance of our world
so round & smooth you could only briefly
be protected from the catch
of serrated things from the *stab of worldlings*
So come you pierced
torn & riven of soul
come you born to trouble
muddled by sunderings & you
so hard pressed
come to the one who offers rest

SO OUGHT WE

after Thomas Traherne

As a seedling grows   toward the sun
As the flame's tongue hungers   once the fire's begun

As wildflowers bloom   for wonder's sake
As migrating geese settle   onto the lake

As the rising tide   is drawn by the moon
As the waiting woman wants   this over soon

As a child in utero   is drawn toward birth
As cloud-released raindrops   fall toward earth

As splattering rain drains   toward the river
As a grateful heart   is drawn toward the giver

As the wolf's eye   is drawn toward sheep
As the weary child   drifts into sleep

As a ship in the storm   makes for the coast
As a man's eyes go   to the one he loves most

Not by wheels   or feet   but a journey of the soul
the poet   carried by desire   is made whole

TWO TYPES OF IBEX

with thanks to David Attenborough & the BBC

There are those who believe in resurrection
& those who don't   (people   that is
I'm talking about people)   & those
rodeo cowgirls   in cliché clothes
untangling lassoes of their own
They lift their eyes toward mountains
Where might their help come from?
It's unthinkable   to think
of the Athabasca Glacier
dripping down to nothing
though all it needs for rebirth
is a new ice age   hard to imagine
the Egyptians   Incas   & Inuit
inventing the same proofless premise
It's like the instinct newborn ibex get
of how to bound along sheer slopes
& how they know
the pretty red fox   is *not*
their friend   There are two types
of ibex   those who thirst for the water
a thousand feet down   & those
already drinking

FRAME

with a tip of the hat to Joseph Beaumont

My human frame
though small when compared
with rhinos & hippos

contains some sixty thousand
miles   of vessels
circulating blood

That's twice the Earth's girth
worth of skinny tubes
Although   as my body's

most obvious tenant   I find
it's far larger   on the inside
than it might   otherwise   seem

an ocean   the rivers
can never fill   a vastness
the whole world never will

My mind holds near & distant cities
& various landscapes   preserving
their moods

& my heart   since it swells
with contradictions
contains multitudes

Ignore the outward appearance
Within these fleshy   temple walls
mysteriously   the Infinite dwells

SYMPATHY

You never did   introduce yourself
kept your distance   like some gothic
cormorant   in the top of a tree
surveying the scene by stealth   With
the aftertaste of defeat   & a wealth
of deceit   on the tip of your tongue
you drew near   your revenge yet
unspent   Taking on the form of a
serpent   you felt it advantageous
to remain anonymous
But were you really unseen?
                    really intervening?
                  really able to do him damage
by polluting virgin shores?
really able to bring the whole
house down   if it couldn't be yours?

I can't say   I'm pleased to meet you
but the game you play's a puzzle
   As lies dripped from your lips
   you laughed at the blunder
      of naive innocence

but did you never wonder
why Omnipotence
made it so easy to slip
creation from his grip?

I'll try to have courtesy
& sympathy
but mostly I've only pity
for when you made paradise
resemble a twilit necropolis
of tilting stones & decaying bones
when you shoved that man of
sorrows into the pit you'd dug
for his children
when you took the bait
& concocted death
you inadvertently opened in our
hearts a desire for what you'd stolen away
& provided a way for the universe
to expand & the insurpassable name
like a flaming fire
to be lifted even higher

COUNTY ARMAGH 1976

In January   early comes the dark
earlier still amid midwinter rain
Now that our textile factory shift is through
sixteen of us cram in for the ride home
We talk of teams   the minibus rolls out
Competing football loyalties support
various clubs   & still we're mates   We stop
& four get out in darkness   Soon our talk
turns to what happened near here yesterday
six Catholics shot dead   three here in Whitecross

Though I'm the only Catholic in the van
as Mowhan Road jostles us side to side
I feel no awkwardness as we discuss
We all agree the Troubles trouble us
Ahead   a red lamp swings to signal stop
We're not surprised   security's grown tight
but as we stop my stomach starts to lurch
The armed men in the rain have faces hid
We're ordered out   lined up along the road
The one of you who's Catholic   step out here

The men on either side, they squeeze my hands
as if to say *We'll not betray you mate*
but still the leader figures I'm that one
I step out trembling fearing for my life
Get down the road he barks *& don't look back*
In black confusion I begin to run
& I run blindly stumbling down the road
as automatic rifle blasts explode
I turn to see the bodies on the ground
The gunmen reload for a second round

—seven—

"Joy shall be joined with all your sorrow here . . ."

—Elizabeth Melville, Lady Culross

LOVE LIKE AN OCEAN (Metaphysicals XIV)

Batter my boat   Wide-spread Water
make your breakers shake my hull
& threaten to capsize me   Push
my bow   & blow me back

attack me broadside   with your
whipping wind   bend
my ambivalence into passion   mend
my apathy   so my heart is full

& don't let me defend
my indefensible complacency
through foolish reason
Knock me overboard   into depths

too great for me   so I   am so thrown
upon your mercy   that as you drag my
drenched form onto your rocky beach
I will know   that you are good

LOVE (3½)

after George Herbert

Despite the evidence   my soul drew back
                                        not trusting
my own experience   my soul grew slack
cautious   hesitant   afraid to play the fool
uncool amid the sophisticates

& yet   Love bade me welcome
                                        though my soul   knowing
my march to every drum   my lack
to every measure   my conspicuous flaws
                                        clearly showing
I would buckle under pressure   prove
a detriment to the cause

Despite the odds   quick-eyed Love
smoothed my wrinkling brow
                                        & soothed me saying
You're ready now

RELEASE (Metaphysicals XV)

If when the end has ended   & all
that's been running down   begins to rewind
until each beginning has once more begun
imagine
the mountains grown taller   more jagged
the lightning-splintered pine
scarless & whole   shining in the sun
even the crumbling Gardiner Expressway
better than on ribbon-cutting day   (not that by then
we'd need it anyway)
your love for God   deeper
than when your rescue song was sung
the chair where the kidnapper held you
suddenly empty   balls of duct tape on the floor
the soiled mattress of imprisonment
rain-soaked   out the back door
If all that's ever been lost   stolen
or shattered   might be returned   redeemed   repaired
(or at least those things worth regaining)
friendships renewed
& the resurrected
looking up with recognition

as bones   are joyfully reformed

from dust   reconnecting

with ligaments   restored

    then *digest   my soul   this*

wholesome meditation

    let the Spirit   the Spirit of God   remind us

of all Christ's done to unbind us

INHERITANCE (Metaphysicals XVI)

From my mother   blue eyes
   watching from the fringes
   like a rabbit   in long grass

From my father   thin brows
   raised & veering   with dreams
   & schemes

From my heavenly Master
   good hunger
From the Spirit   a call
From the Son   his death's conquest
   an eternity of deep love
   & green pastures

BEGINNING & BEGINNING

after John Donne's "Death's Duel"

Can we account for our
becoming   our souls breathed
into tiny bodies   by divine breath?

Did God weave soul   into the fabric
of your embryo   to protect it
from being broken?

Each response from your tongue
when spoken   has its beginning
on your exhaled breath

Every breath   rising from our lungs
is a gift   we lift
along with every song we're singing

Though soul is far more
than the breath we breathe
& spirit far more than the soul

we receive all three   thankfully
each an intricate part
of the whole

Yet   when Christ faced death
& released   unseen   all three
into the Father's hands

(spirit   soul   & final breath)
he knew that's where
they'd always been

LAST DEBT (Metaphysicals XVII)

So many   of those I've loved
have paid their last debt
to nature   My prayers
changed nothing   though I'd set
my heart on changing God
Eyes heavenward   I get
caught in the conundrum
certain   they've met
the divine presence
            & yet
when speaking of death's
short sleep   I forget
resurrection is two-tiered
& I don't have to sweat
my imagination's limitations
of molecules reconfiguring   or let
sentiment make me linger graveside
filled with regret

My soul's eager to see
    those who've gone before
but to see you   my Lord
    so much more

GLISTEN (Metaphysicals XVIII)

She stands
on her hill's height
sure to cause sensation
a cinematic wind
sweeps her hair back
like a declaration   echoing
shore to shore
though you've chosen
her   & want to make
her glisten
At her mirror
in the half-light of her hall
she studies her complexion
Does she see what
must be washed away?
She's so slow to listen
it would be easy   to
dismiss her
Show me
dear Christ   your bride
flawless   bright   & clear
Let me see you kiss her

ANY SUCH TREE (Metaphysicals XIX)

How vexing to be like a tree   planted
to produce sweet apples   yet on whose
grafted branches   crab apples grow

I know   it's unlikely any other orchard
has any such tree   but consider when
ample blossoms bloom

so attractively   how hard they'd be
to prune   I seek you through your silence
until my prayers go mute

unsure whether to value orchard flowers
or only fruit   I bow low then distractedly
turn   a flame that should burn hotter

a mountain spring   spewing
brackish water   a day in May filled
with snow   On my best days

contrite & forgiven   I look less at what
I try to do   & more   dear Jesus   to you

LITANY FOR THE THIRD MILLENIUM

—1—

We reach beyond our reach
to the reaching unreachable
who alone reaches us
whose love endures forever
to the unseen Father the unmade maker
of the perceivable & inconceivable
of all that has been made both whole & broken
whose love endures forever
to the Lamb spoken before our world was made
the sure Word our ears can never contain
the rejected stone blocking our way
whose love endures forever
to the mysterious Ghost overflowing
our bodies & bones with living water
revitalizing our ruinous dejected clay
whose love endures forever
to the unnumbered three the Trinity
lifting us with muscle heart & mind
eternally beyond what intellects could ever find
whose love endures forever

—2—

With the eyes & arms   & insight you've given
we reach   beyond our reach   toward you   Lord
in need of every help you give
grant us heavenly understanding
Through your scriptures   which we've studied
& erroneously muddied   teach us to turn
from twisting them   to being untwisted by them
grant us heavenly understanding
Through your other book   (written in nature)
which we've also trampled   enlighten us
with the light of who you are
grant us heavenly understanding

—3—

When we cry   to you   concerning friends
whose griefs are hard to bear
Lord   hear & answer our prayer
When they face family strife   job loss
weakness   cancer   despair
Lord   hear & answer our prayer
When we cry   to you   concerning victims
of disaster   violence   & warfare
Lord   hear & answer our prayer
When we forgive others   though their wrongs

against us   make forgiveness hard to declare

Lord   hear & answer our prayer

When your Spirit intercedes   with words
we don't know how to pray

Lord   hear & answer our prayer

When friends who've been taught
your way   go astray

Lord   hear & answer our prayer

Even when   through our action   or inaction
we know we share the blame

Lord   hear & answer our prayer

When we pray in the name of the Son
& pray   your will be done   we declare

Lord   hear & answer our prayer

—4—

When we block your light
so our shimmer might show

Lord   have mercy

When our churches fill
with our wearying shadow

Lord   have mercy

When we seek our own glory
trying to prove we are right
when we wander through the night

when we're distracted from your light
which our darkness can never overcome
because   you
        Lord   have mercy
As we seek your face   & nest
in your grace   we know
even when the might of darkness
seems bright   your shine is supreme
& you
        Lord   have mercy

—5—

When we consider   your love opened you
to take on human form
to live as a refugee   an itinerant   a servant
        may we live your truth
        through love for one another
When we consider   your love opened you
to befriend exploited women   tax collectors
the wounded   widows   & fishermen
        may we live your truth
        through love for one another
When we consider   your love opened you
to patience   with disciples   slow to believe
but quick to abandon you in your need

may we live your truth

through love for one another

When we consider   your love opened you

to refrain from retaliating   when you arose

victorious   from the dead

may we live your truth

through love for one another

May we turn to you   Lord

rather than to all you can do for us

May we praise your name   Lord

rather than thoughtlessly repeating words

May we bring you glory   Lord

rather than to ourselves   or even to our churches

May these things come to be

Amen

—appendix—

John Donne's Holy Sonnets

JOHN DONNE'S HOLY SONNET I

Thou hast made me, and shall Thy work decay?
Repair me now, for now mine end doth haste;
I run to death, and Death meets me as fast,
And all my pleasures are like yesterday.
I dare not move my dim eyes any way;
Despair behind, and Death before doth cast
Such terror, and my feeble flesh doth waste
By sin in it, which it towards hell doth weigh.
Only Thou art above, and when towards Thee
By Thy leave I can look, I rise again;
But our old subtle foe so tempteth me,
That not one hour myself I can sustain.
Thy grace may wing me to prevent his art
And thou like adamant draw mine iron heart.

JOHN DONNE'S HOLY SONNET II

As due by many titles I resign
Myself to thee, O God, first I was made
By Thee, and for Thee, and when I was decay'd
Thy blood bought that, the which before was Thine.
I am Thy son, made with Thyself to shine,
Thy servant, whose pains Thou hast still repaid,
Thy sheep, Thine image, and—till I betray'd
Myself—a temple of Thy Spirit divine.
Why doth the devil then usurp on me?
Why doth he steal, nay ravish, that's Thy right?
Except Thou rise and for Thine own work fight,
O! I shall soon despair, when I shall see
That Thou lovest mankind well, yet wilt not choose me,
And Satan hates me, yet is loth to lose me.

JOHN DONNE'S HOLY SONNET III

O! might those sighs and tears return again
Into my breast and eyes, which I have spent,
That I might in this holy discontent
Mourn with some fruit, as I have mourn'd in vain.
In mine Idolatry what showers of rain
Mine eyes did waste? what griefs my heart did rent?

That sufferance was my sin, I now repent;
'Cause I did suffer, I must suffer pain.
Th' hydroptic drunkard, and night-scouting thief,
The itchy lecher, and self-tickling proud
Have the remembrance of past joys, for relief
Of coming ills. To poor me is allow'd
No ease; for long, yet vehement grief hath been
Th' effect and cause, the punishment and sin.

JOHN DONNE'S HOLY SONNET IV

O, my black soul, now thou art summoned
By sickness, Death's herald and champion;
Thou'rt like a pilgrim, which abroad hath done
Treason, and durst not turn to whence he's fled;
Or like a thief, which till death's doom be read,
Wisheth himself deliver'd from prison,
But damn'd and haled to execution,
Wisheth that still he might be imprisoned.
Yet grace, if thou repent, thou canst not lack;
But who shall give thee that grace to begin?
O, make thyself with holy mourning black,
And red with blushing, as thou art with sin;
Or wash thee in Christ's blood, which hath this might,
That being red, it dyes red souls to white.

JOHN DONNE'S HOLY SONNET V

I am a little world made cunningly
Of elements, and an angelic sprite;
But black sin hath betray'd to endless night
My world's both parts, and, O, both parts must die.
You which beyond that heaven which was most high
Have found new spheres, and of new land can write,
Pour new seas in mine eyes, that so I might
Drown my world with my weeping earnestly,
Or wash it if it must be drown'd no more.
But O, it must be burnt; alas! the fire
Of lust and envy burnt it heretofore,
And made it fouler; let their flames retire,
And burn me, O Lord, with a fiery zeal
Of Thee and Thy house, which doth in eating heal.

JOHN DONNE'S HOLY SONNET VI

This is my play's last scene; here heavens appoint
My pilgrimage's last mile; and my race
Idly, yet quickly run, hath this last pace;
My span's last inch, my minute's latest point;
And gluttonous Death will instantly unjoint
My body and soul, and I shall sleep a space;

But my ever-waking part shall see that face,
Whose fear already shakes my every joint.
Then, as my soul to heaven her first seat takes flight,
And earth-born body in the earth shall dwell,
So fall my sins, that all may have their right,
To where they're bred and would press me to hell.
Impute me righteous, thus purged of evil,
For thus I leave the world, the flesh, the devil.

JOHN DONNE'S HOLY SONNET VII

At the round earth's imagined corners blow
Your trumpets, angels, and arise, arise
From death, you numberless infinities
Of souls, and to your scattered bodies go;
All whom the flood did, and fire shall o'erthrow,
All whom war, dea[r]th, age, agues, tyrannies,
Despair, law, chance hath slain, and you, whose eyes
Shall behold God, and never taste death's woe.
But let them sleep, Lord, and me mourn a space;
For, if above all these my sins abound,
'Tis late to ask abundance of Thy grace,
When we are there. Here on this lowly ground,
Teach me how to repent, for that's as good
As if Thou hadst seal'd my pardon with Thy blood.

JOHN DONNE'S HOLY SONNET VIII

If faithful souls be alike glorified
As angels, then my father's soul doth see,
And adds this even to full felicity,
That valiantly I hell's wide mouth o'erstride.
But if our minds to these souls be descried
By circumstances, and by signs that be
Apparent in us not immediately,
How shall my mind's white truth by them be tried?
They see idolatrous lovers weep and mourn,
And stile blasphemous conjurers to call
On Jesu's name, and pharisaical
Dissemblers feign devotion. Then turn,
O pensive soul, to God, for He knows best
Thy grief, for He put it into my breast.

JOHN DONNE'S HOLY SONNET IX

If poisonous minerals, and if that tree,
Whose fruit threw death on (else immortal) us,
If lecherous goats, if serpents envious
Cannot be damn'd, alas ! why should I be?
Why should intent or reason, born in me,

Make sins, else equal, in me more heinous?
And, mercy being easy, and glorious
To God, in His stern wrath why threatens He?
But who am I, that dare dispute with Thee?
O God, O! of Thine only worthy blood,
And my tears, make a heavenly Lethean flood,
And drown in it my sin's black memory.
That Thou remember them, some claim as debt;
I think it mercy if Thou wilt forget.

JOHN DONNE'S HOLY SONNET X

Death be not proud, though some have callèd thee
Mighty and dreadfull, for, thou art not so,
For, those, whom thou think'st, thou dost overthrow,
Die not, poore death, nor yet canst thou kill me.
From rest and sleepe, which but thy pictures bee,
Much pleasure, then from thee, much more must flow,
And soonest our best men with thee doe goe,
Rest of their bones, and soules deliverie.
Thou art slave to Fate, Chance, kings, and desperate men,
And dost with poyson, warre, and sicknesse dwell,
And poppie, or charmes can make us sleepe as well,
And better than thy stroake; why swell'st thou then;
One short sleepe past, wee wake eternally,
And death shall be no more, death, thou shalt die.

JOHN DONNE'S HOLY SONNET XI

Spit in my face, you Jews, and pierce my side,
Buffet, and scoff, scourge, and crucify me,
For I have sinn'd, and sinne', and only He,
Who could do no iniquity, hath died.
But by my death can not be satisfied
My sins, which pass the Jews' impiety.
They kill'd once an inglorious man, but I
Crucify him daily, being now glorified.
O let me then His strange love still admire;
Kings pardon, but He bore our punishment;
And Jacob came clothed in vile harsh attire,
But to supplant, and with gainful intent;
God clothed Himself in vile man's flesh, that so
He might be weak enough to suffer woe.

JOHN DONNE'S HOLY SONNET XII

Why are we by all creatures waited on?
Why do the prodigal elements supply
Life and food to me, being more pure than I,
Simpler and further from corruption?
Why brook'st thou, ignorant horse, subjection?
Why dost thou, bull and boar, so sillily

Dissemble weakness, and by one man's stroke die,
Whose whole kind you might swallow and feed upon?
Weaker I am, woe's me, and worse than you;
You have not sinn'd, nor need be timorous.
But wonder at a greater, for to us
Created nature doth these things subdue;
But their Creator, whom sin, nor nature tied,
For us, His creatures, and His foes, hath died.

JOHN DONNE'S HOLY SONNET XIII

What if this present were the world's last night?
Mark in my heart, O soul, where thou dost dwell,
The picture of Christ crucified, and tell
Whether His countenance can thee affright.
Tears in His eyes quench the amazing light;
Blood fills his frowns, which from His pierced head fell;
And can that tongue adjudge thee unto hell,
Which pray'd forgiveness for His foes' fierce spite?
No, no ; but as in my idolatry
I said to all my profane mistresses,
Beauty of pity, foulness only is
A sign of rigour ; so I say to thee,
To wicked spirits are horrid shapes assign'd;
This beauteous form assures a piteous mind.

JOHN DONNE'S HOLY SONNET XIV

Batter my heart, three-person'd God; for you
As yet but knock; breathe, shine, and seek to mend;
That I may rise, and stand, o'erthrow me, and bend
Your force, to break, blow, burn, and make me new.
I, like an usurp'd town, to another due,
Labour to admit you, but O, to no end.
Reason, your viceroy in me, me should defend,
But is captived, and proves weak or untrue.
Yet dearly I love you, and would be loved fain,
But am betroth'd unto your enemy:
Divorce me, untie, or break that knot again,
Take me to you, imprison me, for I,
Except you enthrall me, never shall be free,
Nor ever chaste, except you ravish me.

JOHN DONNE'S HOLY SONNET XV

Wilt thou love God as he thee? then digest,
My soul, this wholesome meditation,
How God the Spirit, by angels waited on
In heaven, doth make His temple in thy breast.
The Father having begot a Son most blest,
And still begetting—for he ne'er begun—

Hath deign'd to choose thee by adoption,
Co-heir to His glory, and Sabbath's endless rest.
And as a robb'd man, which by search doth find
His stolen stuff sold, must lose or buy it again,
The Sun of glory came down, and was slain,
Us whom He had made, and Satan stole, to unbind.
'Twas much, that man was made like God before,
But, that God should be made like man, much more.

JOHN DONNE'S HOLY SONNET XVI

Father, part of His double interest
Unto Thy kingdom Thy Son gives to me;
His jointure in the knotty Trinity
He keeps, and gives to me his death's conquest.
This Lamb, whose death with life the world hath blest,
Was from the world's beginning slain, and He
Hath made two wills, which with the legacy
Of His and Thy kingdom do thy sons invest.
Yet such are these laws, that men argue yet
Whether a man those statutes can fulfil.
None doth; but thy all-healing grace and Spirit
Revive again what law and letter kill.
Thy law's abridgement, and Thy last command
Is all but love; Oh let this last Will stand!

JOHN DONNE'S HOLY SONNET XVII

Since she whom I loved hath paid her last debt
To Nature, and to hers, and my good is dead,
And her soul early into heaven ravishèd,
Wholly on heavenly things my mind is set.
Here the admiring her my mind did whet
To seek thee, God; so streams do show the head;
But though I have found thee, and thou my thirst hast fed,
A holy thirsty dropsy melts me yet.
But why should I beg more love, when as thou
Dost woo my soul, for hers offering all thine:
And dost not only fear lest I allow
My love to saints and angels, things divine,
But in thy tender jealousy dost doubt
Lest the world, flesh, yea, devil put thee out.

JOHN DONNE'S HOLY SONNET XVIII

Show me, dear Christ, thy spouse so bright and clear.
What! is it she which on the other shore
Goes richly painted? or which, robbed and tore,
Laments and mourns in Germany and here?
Sleeps she a thousand, then peeps up one year?
Is she self-truth, and errs? now new, now outwore?

Doth she, and did she, and shall she evermore
On one, on seven, or on no hill appear?
Dwells she with us, or like adventuring knights
First travel we to seek, and then make love?
Betray, kind husband, thy spouse to our sights,
And let mine amorous soul court thy mild dove,
Who is most true and pleasing to thee then
When she is embraced and open to most men.

JOHN DONNE'S HOLY SONNET XIX

Oh, to vex me, contraries meet in one:
Inconstancy unnaturally hath begot
A constant habit; that when I would not
I change in vows, and in devotion.
As humorous is my contrition
As my profane love, and as soon forgot:
As riddlingly distempered, cold and hot,
As praying, as mute; as infinite, as none.
I durst not view heaven yesterday; and today
In prayers and flattering speeches I court God:
Tomorrow I quake with true fear of his rod.
So my devout fits come and go away
Like a fantastic ague; save that here
Those are my best days, when I shake with feare.

acknowledgements

The centre around which this poetry collection is built consists of nineteen poems which I call the Metaphysicals; they are my interactions with the nineteen Holy Sonnets of Anglican cleric John Donne (1572–1631). I would like to thank Rose Postma, Poetry Editor of *Reformed Journal*, who agreed to publish all nineteen of my Metaphysicals serially over nineteen months from January 2023 to July 2024. Such an unprecedented vote of confidence for my poetry cannot be taken for granted, nor can I thank her enough.

I would also like to thank the editors of the following publications where the remaining poems have appeared, sometimes in slightly different forms.

Alliance Connection — "Stargazer"

Amethyst Review — "The World's Sharpness"

Anglican Theological Review — "Chorus of the Splendid Poison Frog"

Arts: The Arts in Religious and Theological Studies — "Implement"

The Christian Century — "You Could Have Made," "Mercies," "A Window"

Crux — "Simeon"

Cumberland River Review — "New Life," Watcher of the Fields"

Ekstasis — "Poem for a Time of Crisis," "Line & Colour," "Sympathy"

Evangelical Review of Theology — "Curved Beauty," "Frame"

Event — "As She Flew Past," "Miles To Go"

Faith Today — "Palmless Sunday"

Fare Forward — "This Coronet," "Two Types of Ibex"

Fathom — "Sargassum"

First Things — "Shepherd," "Peregrine Falcon"

Foreshadow — "Inferno," "Ruins Remind Us," "Beginning & Beginning"

Innisfree Poetry Journal — "County Armagh 1976"

The Irish Times — "Kitty Stobbling Dances On"

Literary Review of Canada — "The Change"

Mockingbird — "Osprey"

Presence — "I Draw in Dust a Circle with my Foot"

Quadrant (Australia) — "Love (3½)"

Queen's Quarterly — "Birdwatching with Confucius"

Relief — "Riff on Traherne," "Poem Arising from a Line by Herbert"

Sojourners — "Another Ampersand (+&)"

Solum Journal — "Reflection on Shakespeare's Sonnet 146"

Theology (UK) — "Prayer Without Answer"

Traces Journal — "Cardinal Virtues"

Transpositions (UK) — "Climatology with Augustine"

Vision — "So Ought We"

The Windhover — "A Poet Available for God's Service," "Prayer"

Windsor Review — "Owl Heart"

The poem "Two Types of Ibex" was the winner of the 2022 *Fare Forward* Poetry Competition. At that time it was called "Two Types of Ibeks," however my friend, the impressive copy editor Debbie Sawczak, pointed out that although *Ibeks* does frequently appear on the internet, the correct term is *Ibex* (singular) and *ibex, ibexes* or *ibices* (plural). Besides Debbie, who actually knew that?

"Litany for the Third Millennium" first appeared on the website of the Christian & Missionary Alliance (Canada) in order to make it freely available for use in churches.

"Poem for a Time of Crisis" was reprinted in *Orchards Poetry Journal.*

"Implement" was also subsequently included in the Singapore-based anthology *A Given Grace* (Squircle Line Press, 2021).

"As She Flew Past" was reposted at *Poetry Pause* by the League of Canadian Poets.

"Two Types of Ibex," "Radiant (Metaphysicals II)," and "You Could Have Made" also appeared in *Secularism and the Pursuit of Transcendence* (edited by Stanley E. Porter and Wendy J. Porter), as part of my essay "Poetry & the Transcendent" (Wipf & Stock, 2024).

The first public reading of my poem "Last Debt (Metaphysicals XVII)" was on June first, 2024, at *A Gathering of Remembrance* for Marion Franklin (1943–2024) at Little Trinity Anglican Church, Toronto.

I would like to thank Ryan Apple and the members of his "Kingdom Poets" critique group, which arose out of my anthology *In a Strange Land: Introducing Ten Kingdom Poets* (Poiema/Cascade, 2019). Several of the poems in this present book were improved through the input of poets from this collective.

Others whom I feel the need to acknowledge as a blessing to me and my poetry include John & Marion Franklin (Imago), David Kent & Margo Swiss (St. Thomas Poetry Series), Stan & Wendy Porter (McMaster Divinity College), John Van Rys (Redeemer University), and of course my loving wife, Gloria, and our family.

Soli Deo Gloria

other books by D.S. Martin

So the Moon Would Not Be Swallowed (2007 — chapbook)

Poiema (2008)

Conspiracy of Light: Poems Inspired by the Legacy of C.S. Lewis (2013)

Ampersand (2018)

Angelicus (2021)

Anthologies:

The Turning Aside: The Kingdom Poets Book of Contemporary Christian Poetry (2016)

Adam, Eve, & the Riders of the Apocalypse: 39 Contemporary Poets on the Characters of the Bible (2017)

In a Strange Land: Introducing Ten Kingdom Poets (2019)

about Paraclete Press

Paraclete Press is the publishing arm of the Cape Cod Benedictine community, the Community of Jesus. Presenting a full expression of Christian belief and practice, we reflect the ecumenical charism of the Community and its dedication to sacred music, the fine arts, and the written word.

SCAN TO READ MORE

www.paracletepress.com

O that my words were written down!
O that they were inscribed in a book!
O that with an iron pen and with lead
they were engraved on a rock forever!
—JOB 19:23–24

Outcast and utterly alone, Job pours out his anguish to his Maker. From the depths of his pain, he reveals a trust in God's goodness that is stronger than his despair, giving humanity some of the most beautiful and poetic verses of all time. Paraclete's Iron Pen imprint is inspired by this spirit of unvarnished honesty and tenacious hope.

BOOKS FROM THE IRON PEN IMPRINT

Contemporary Catholic Poetry edited by April Lindner and Ryan Wilson

Glory in the Margins by Nikki Grimes

Taking Root in the Heart edited by Jill Peláez Baumgaertner

To Shatter Glass by Sister Sharon Hunter

Angels Everywhere by Luci Shaw

Christian Poetry in America Since 1940 edited by Micah Mattix and Sally Thomas

Holy Land by Angela Alaimo O'Donnell

Which Seeds Will Grow by Andrew Callis

Glory, Too by Nikki Grimes

An Incremental Life by Luci Shaw

you may also enjoy . . .